This journal belongs to

· ·

You ou are a beautiful child of God, precious to Him in every way.
As you seek Him, He will listen to the prayers of your heart
and fill Your quiet time with His peace.

This journal has been divided into nine themed sections
based on some of the most common prayer requests.
Within each section we have gathered prayers, promises,
and praises for those issues closest to your heart.
Let this journal inspire you to record your personal prayers,
express your thoughts, embrace your dreams,
and listen to what God is saying to you.

*I love the LORD because he
hears my voice and my prayer....
Because he bends down to listen,
I will pray as long as I have breath!*
PSALM 116:1-2 NLT

My Quiet Time

PRAYER JOURNAL

Ellie Claire
gift & paper expressions

...inspired by life

SECTION ONE

Guide My Path

Many of us have our lives planned out. Some of us want the American dream of education, travel, career, marriage, kids, and retirement. There are those who want to make it big while others prefer to quietly serve those in need. Some simply crave contentment. And then there are those who hope to set the world on fire.

God has a plan too. Sometimes His plan resembles ours. Sometimes it doesn't. But His plan is always bigger and better than anything we can plan for ourselves. He asks us to trust our future, our plans, our every decision to His guidance.

As we make the daily decisions that affect the path of our lives, these prayers, promises, and praises can help us trust our Guide and the plans He has for us.

Plans for the Future

Dear Lord,
As I look toward the future
Bright hope conducts this prayer,
For I know the plans You have for me
Were wrought with divine care....
Your Word will be a lamp for me,
A guide to light my way,
A solid place to set my feet,
A compass when I stray....
Dear Lord, show me Your favor,
At all times keep me blessed,
May Your face ever shine upon me,
With peace and perfect rest.
Amen.

MARY FAIRCHILD

Joy comes from knowing God loves me and knows who I am
and where I'm going...that my future is secure as I rest in Him.

DR. JAMES DOBSON

"For I know the plans I have for you," declares the LORD,
"plans to prosper you and not to harm you,
plans to give you hope and a future."

JEREMIAH 29:11 NIV

God specializes in things fresh and firsthand.
His plans for you this year may outshine those of the past....
He's preparing to fill your days with reasons to give Him praise.

JONI EARECKSON TADA

prayers

promises

praise

When Plans Change

Dear Father,
Thank You for holding me in Your hands no matter
where I am. You amaze me. You have things set in place
before I even know I need them.

But, Lord, just when I thought I was getting my act together,
the scene changed. Here I am in a new situation needing
your steady guidance again. How do I move forward?
What choices do I make? Please reveal to me the next step.

I trust that no matter where the path leads,
You will be there before me. You are here, there,
everywhere—even on the far side of the sea.
I pray that You will help me accept the changes that come,
that You will fill me with contentment in every situation,
every location. Remind me today that You are the One
in charge of my plans. You have everything under control.
All I need to do is trust. Amen.

If I rise on the wings of the dawn,
if I settle on the far side of the sea,
even there your hand will guide me,
your right hand will hold me fast.

PSALM 139:9-10 NIV

He's in control of our lives; nothing lies outside the realm of His
redemptive grace. Even when we make mistakes, fail in relationships,
or deliberately make bad choices, God can redeem us.

PENELOPE J. STOKES

prayers

promises

praise

God's Guidance

Lord,
You are my guide. Because I have You,
I have everything I need. You lull me to sleep in gentle meadows.
You give me water from pure, bubbling streams. You refresh my
soul. You guide me to the right path. I'd be lost without You.

Even when I am surrounded by evil, help me to not be afraid.
Show me the way out. Keep reminding me that You are right
beside me. Comfort me and keep me safe and secure.
Lord, You spread out all my favorite foods just for me
as my enemies look on. You give me Your blessing.
No matter how much I drink, my cup is always full.

Lord, guide my life to good and beautiful things. Give me grace.
And help me to follow You all the days of my life. Amen.

PARAPHRASE OF PSALM 23

After a hard day scrambling to find your way around the world,
it's assuring to come home to a place you know. God can be equally
familiar to you. With time you can learn where to go for nourishment,
where to hide for protection, where to turn for guidance.

MAX LUCADO

The LORD will guide you always;
he will satisfy your needs in a sun-scorched land

ISAIAH 58:11 NIV

prayers

promises

praise

Build My House

How great you are, O Sovereign LORD!
There is no one like you. We have never even heard of another
God like you!... You made a great name for yourself when you
redeemed your people from Egypt. You performed awesome
miracles and drove out the nations and gods that stood in their
way. And now, O LORD God, I am your servant; do as you have
promised concerning me and my family. Confirm it as a promise
that will last forever. And may your name be honored forever....

I have been bold enough to pray this prayer to you
because you have revealed all this to your servant, saying,
"I will build a house for you...." For you are God, O Sovereign
LORD. Your words are truth, and you have promised these good
things to your servant. And now, may it please you to bless the
house of your servant, so that it may continue forever before
you. For you have spoken, and when you grant a blessing to your
servant, O Sovereign LORD, it is an eternal blessing!

2 SAMUEL 7:22-23, 25-29 NLT

Anybody can build a house;
we need the Lord for the creation of a home.

JOHN HENRY JOWETT

God does not want us to build our lives on anything that can be lost;
only on the eternal, unchanging Lord.

ALEC BROOKS

prayers

promises

praise

Direct My Decisions

Thank You, Father,
for all Your guidance.
I am in awe of how You use my stumblings to further
Your divine plan. Father, help me with the hard decisions
in my life. So many days I am overwhelmed, not knowing
what to do. I'm so afraid of the responsibility of my choices,
of making a mistake, that I put off making a decision.
I need Your continued guidance.

Give me courage to make the decisions that have to be made.
Help me to overcome my fear and indecision.
Push me in the direction You want me to go.
Open my mind to the right path and give me
the strength to follow it with confidence even if I'm afraid.
Let my choices always glorify You. Amen.

Let the morning bring me word of your unfailing love,
for I have put my trust in you. Show me the way I should go.

Psalm 143:8 niv

Should we feel at times disheartened and discouraged,
a simple movement of heart toward God will renew our powers.
Whatever He may demand of us, He will give us at the moment
the strength and courage that we need.

François Fénelon

prayers

promises

praise

Advice from Friends

Dear Lord,
I am so grateful for the friends You have put in my life.
You have given me the kind of friends who are not only fun,
loyal, and considerate, but who also make me a better person.
I praise You for showing Your care for me by surrounding
me with inspiring people who rely on Your Word and the
promptings of Your Spirit.

Lord, help me to listen to the friends that give me suggestions
and advice. Use them to guide me on Your path.
Speak truth through them. Open my heart and mind
to find Your voice in their words even if it is difficult to hear.
And when the time comes, help me to give the same studied,
godly advice that I received from them. Amen.

The heartfelt counsel of a friend
is as sweet as perfume and incense.
PROVERBS 27:9 NLT

Who is more indefatiguable in toil, when there is occasion for toil,
than a friend? Who is readier to rejoice in one's good fortune?
Whose praise is sweeter? From whose lips does one learn the truth
with less pain? What fortress, what bulwarks,
what arms are more steadfast than loyal hearts?
JOHN CHRYSOSTOM

prayers

promises

praise

Giving Control to God

Father,
I abandon myself into Your hands;
do with me what You will.
Whatever You may do, I thank You:
I am ready for all, I accept all.
Let only Your will be done in me,
and in all Your creatures—
I wish no more than this, O Lord.
Into Your hands I commend my soul;
I offer it to You with all the love of my heart,
for I love You, Lord,
and so need to give myself,
to surrender myself into Your hands,
without reserve,
and with boundless confidence,
for You are my Father.

CHARLES DE FOUCAULD

Abandon yourself to His care and guidance,
as a sheep in the care of a shepherd, and trust Him utterly.

HANNAH WHITALL SMITH

Commit to the LORD whatever you do,
and he will establish your plans.

PROVERBS 16:3 NIV

prayers

promises

praise

God's Guiding Word

Your Word is a map for our journey through life,
Lord. You've marked the pitfalls, offered advice,
and given us examples of what to do and not do.
Oh, how I need that direction, that compass guiding my steps.

Help me to turn to Scripture before I make any decision.
Help me to let the inspired words sink deep into my life.
Your Word is full of knowledge and wisdom.
It has answers to questions I haven't yet thought to ask.
It shows me the way like a lighthouse guides ships
to safety through stormy seas.

God, thank You for the light of Your Word. Through it,
You have given me hope, guided my steps, and built
my confidence. Help me to seek that light today. Amen.

Your commandments give me understanding;
no wonder I hate every false way of life.
Your word is a lamp to guide my feet
and a light for my path.
I've promised it once, and I'll promise it again:
I will obey your righteous regulations.

PSALM 119:104–106 NLT

God's Word acts as a light for our paths. It can help scare off
unwanted thoughts in our minds and protect us from the enemy.

GARY SMALLEY AND JOHN TRENT

prayers

promises

praise

SECTION TWO
My Daily Bread

When the Hebrew people wandered in the wilderness, God provided food for them daily. *Daily*. A new supply was there for them every morning. They were not allowed to pick up the food and save it for the next day. They were required to rely on Him for their bread one day at a time.

God still wants us to depend on Him daily. In a time when we have refrigerators the size of small countries and storage units that number in the millions, it's tempting to value self-reliance above God-dependence.

But everything we have is from God. Everything. Praying for our daily needs, thanking Him for His forever promises, and praising Him for His abundance are a few ways we can show our gratitude for His everything.

Daily Prayer

In this manner, therefore, pray:
Our Father in heaven,
Hallowed be Your name.
Your kingdom come.
Your will be done
On earth as it is in heaven.
Give us this day our daily bread.
And forgive us our debts,
As we forgive our debtors.
And do not lead us into temptation,
But deliver us from the evil one.
For Yours is the kingdom and the power
and the glory forever. Amen.

MATTHEW 6:9-13 NKJV

Part of our job is simply to be…always attentive to what we are doing
and what is going on inside us, at the same time we listen and pay
attention to the people and events around us. Part of our job is to expect
that, if we are attentive and willing, God will "give us prayer," will give us
the things we need, "our daily bread," to heal and grow in love.

ROBERTA C. BONDI

Don't worry about anything; instead, pray about everything.
Tell God what you need, and thank him for all he has done.

PHILIPPIANS 4:6 NLT

Praise be to the Lord, to God our Savior,
who daily bears our burdens.

PSALM 68:19 NIV

prayers

promises

praise

Daily Food

Lord,
Thank You for my daily bread.
For the breakfasts, lunches, suppers, and snacks.
Thank You for beverages, hot and cold. Thank You for the
abundance on my table, in my cabinets, and on the shelves
of my refrigerator. For every morsel, I thank You. Even when
the morsels are few, I thank You for providing them.

Lord, bless the food to my body.
Thank You for the energy it supplies.
Use that energy for Your glory. Use it to fuel Your work.

Bless the hands that prepared it, packaged it, or served it.
For preparing and providing all that I need, I thank You. Amen.

May this food restore our strength, giving new energy
to tired limbs, new thoughts to weary minds. May this drink
restore our souls, giving new vision to dry spirits,
new warmth to cold hearts. And once refreshed,
may we give new pleasure to You, who gives us all.

IRISH DINNER BLESSING

All creatures look to you
to give them their food at the proper time.
When you give it to them,
they gather it up;
when you open your hand,
they are satisfied with good things.

PSALM 104:27–28 NIV

prayers

promises

praise

Daily Finances

Dear Jesus,
You are so faithful. When I trust You, I am amazed
at what You do with my money. You stretch it and give it
and use it in surprising ways. Help me be generous.
I am so tempted to try to control all the money issues myself.
I often make decisions to the tune of "there is not enough."
But with You there is always enough. You are forever faithful.
Take my "not enough" and multiply it into more than enough.

Jesus, help me to be a faithful giver. When I have choices,
show me the right one. Teach me to not make decisions out of fear,
but out of faithfulness, cheerfulness, and thankfulness. Amen.

Every good and perfect gift is from above,
coming down from the Father of the heavenly lights,
who does not change like shifting shadows.

JAMES 1:17 NIV

Give me neither poverty nor riches!
Give me just enough to satisfy my needs.

PROVERBS 30:8 NLT

Great is Thy faithfulness!
Morning by morning new mercies I see.
All I have needed Thy hand hath provided;
Great is Thy faithfulness, Lord, unto me!

THOMAS CHISHOLM

prayers

promises

praise

Daily Provision

Dear Father,
Thank You for everything You've given me.
You surprise me all the time with just what I need
right when I need it. I love how You do that.
Yet over and over again I forget that and try
to do things myself. When I need something,
I worry, plot, and plan ways to get it.
I tie up the time, energy, and talent I could be using
for You to try to work things out for myself.

The truth is, I don't even know what I need.
I know what I want. I know what the world tells me I need.
I want to make today, Father, the day I rely on You.
You know my true needs and You always provide.
Let me drink in the reality of that. You always provide.
Help me to trust You to provide what is necessary in Your time.
Help me to stop fretting, and doing, and scheming, and rely on
You, wait on You. Thank You for being my Provider. Amen.

God will generously provide all you need. Then you will always have
everything you need and plenty left over to share with others.

2 CORINTHIANS 9:8 NLT

Let everything that has breath praise the LORD.
Praise the LORD.

PSALM 150:6 NIV

prayers

promises

praise

Every Blessing

I Thank Thee
O Thou whose bounty fills my cup,
With every blessing meet!
I give Thee thanks for every drop—
The bitter and the sweet.
I praise Thee for the desert road,
And for the riverside;
For all Thy goodness hath bestowed,
And all Thy grace denied.
I thank Thee for both smile and frown,
And for the gain and loss;
I praise Thee for the future crown
And for the present cross.
I thank Thee for both wings of love
Which stirred my worldly nest;
And for the stormy clouds which drove
Me, trembling, to Thy breast.
I bless Thee for the glad increase,
And for the waning joy;
And for this strange, this settled peace
Which nothing can destroy.

JANE CREWDSON

You go before me and follow me.
You place your hand of blessing on my head.

PSALM 139:5 NLT

prayers

promises

praise

For All He Does

I found the sun for me this morning.
I thank You, Lord.
I found the warm water in the shower.
I praise You.
I found the bread in my kitchen this morning, Lord.
I thank You.
I found the fresh air as I stood outside the door.
I praise You.
For all that I see that You do for me,
I thank You.
For all that I do not see that You do for me,
I praise You.

CHRISTOPHER DE VINCK

Rejoice always, pray continually, give thanks in all circumstances;
for this is God's will for you in Christ Jesus.

1 THESSALONIANS 5:16–18 NIV

Seeing our Father in everything makes life one long thanksgiving
and gives a rest of heart, and, more than that,
a gayety of spirit, that is unspeakable.

HANNAH WHITALL SMITH

I will tell of the kindnesses of the LORD,
the deeds for which he is to be praised,
according to all the LORD has done for us...
according to his compassion and many kindnesses.

ISAIAH 63:7 NIV

prayers

promises

praise

Daily Increase

Dear Father,
I am so grateful for all You have entrusted to me.
Not just things, but talents, health, relationships,
and opportunities. I am guilty of not always using the talent
You've given me. I sometimes squander opportunities.
I often neglect my health. Forgive me.

Make me the kind of person You can trust to take care
of the small and the large gifts I receive from You. Father,
I really want to do things well. Help me to take all You give and
through prayer, hard work, and praise increase Your investment.

Father, Your daily giving is so often taken for granted.
I don't want to do that. Help me to receive with gratefulness
and to use every gift fully, never leaving any part of it unused
or unappreciated. Lead me to where my gifts are most needed.
Help me to share all I have and find more. Bless my gifts.
Use me, Father, for Your glory. Amen.

The master was full of praise. "Well done, my good and faithful servant.
You have been faithful in handling this small amount, so now I will give
you many more responsibilities. Let's celebrate together!"

MATTHEW 25:21 NLT

This most generous God who gives seed to the farmer that becomes
bread for your meals is more than extravagant with you. He gives you
something you can then give away, which grows into full-formed lives,
robust in God, wealthy in every way, so that you can be generous in
every way, producing with us great praise to God.

2 CORINTHIANS 9:10 MSG

prayers

promises

praise

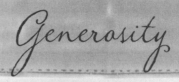

Generosity

Lord Jesus,
teach me to be generous;
teach me to serve You as You deserve,
to give and not to count the cost,
to fight and not to heed the wounds,
to toil and not to seek for rest,
to labor and not to seek reward,
except that of knowing that I do Your will.
Amen.

IGNATIUS LOYOLA

A mark of Christian maturity is actively sharing and growing
in extending the ministry of Christ to others in the world.

JIM BANKHEAD

Real generosity is doing something nice for someone
who'll never find it out.

FRANK A. CLARK

People who deal with life generously and large-heartedly
go on multiplying relationships to the end.

ARTHUR CHRISTOPHER BENSON

Now, our God, we give you thanks, and praise your glorious name.
But who am I, and who are my people, that we should be able to give
as generously as this? Everything comes from you,
and we have given you only what comes from your hand.

1 CHRONICLES 29:13–14 NIV

prayers

promises

praise

SECTION THREE

My Relationships

When it comes down to it, our whole lives are measured by our relationships. Caring and praying for our family, friends, church family, and coworkers takes time and loving attention. We want them to be healthy, happy, and spiritually whole. These are the people we love, depend on, and share life with.

When we take the time to nurture and bring to God those closest to our hearts and bring them to God in prayer, we build eternal bonds. Asking God to watch over them and to gather them close is one of the sweetest gifts we can give our loved ones. And we honor God by entrusting our relationships to His care.

Belonging to God

Jesus looked up to heaven and said,
"Father...my prayer is not for the world, but for those
you have given me, because they belong to you.
All who are mine belong to you, and you have given them to me,
so they bring me glory....

"Now I am coming to you. I told them many things
while I was with them in this world so they would be filled
with my joy. I have given them your word. And the world
hates them because they do not belong to the world,
just as I do not belong to the world. I'm not asking you to take
them out of the world, but to keep them safe from the evil one.
They do not belong to this world any more than I do."

JOHN 17:1, 9–10, 13–16 NLT

When God's Son took on flesh, He truly and bodily took on,
out of pure grace, our being, our nature, ourselves.
This was the eternal counsel of the triune God. Now we are in Him....
We belong to Him because we are in Him.

DIETRICH BONHOEFFER

Our God is so wonderfully good, and lovely,
and blessed in every way that the mere fact of belonging to Him
is enough for an untellable fullness of joy!

HANNAH WHITALL SMITH

prayers

promises

praise

The Blessing of Family

Father,
I come to You in gratitude for blessing me with my family.
Thank You for the gift of them. Lord, I ask that You bless
each one. Bless my spouse, my siblings, my children,
my parents, my in-laws, and those in my extended family.
Touch their lives with special meaning. Watch over each one.

For those who know You, I thank You for their salvation. For those
who haven't come to You yet, please help them find their way into
Your grace. Put people and circumstances in their lives to bring
them and keep them close to You. Show me how to help them.

Bless our relationships with one another. Give us a sense
of belonging to each other and to You. Build bonds between
us that nothing on earth can break. Amen.

Heavenly Father,
Help me build a tradition of communication and conversation within
my family. May our mealtimes become a time of sharing and learning
about each other. Whether we are two or ten in number,
thank You for the blessing of being a part of a family. Amen.

KIM BOYCE

You've blessed my family so that it will continue
in your presence always. Because you have blessed it,
GOD, it's *really* blessed—blessed for good!

1 CHRONICLES 17:27 MSG

prayers

promises

praise

Faithful Friends

Dear God,
What a blessing it is to have a trustworthy friend in
whose heart I can safely hide all my secrets. How comforting
to have someone whose conscience I can depend on almost as
much as my own, who can relieve my cares by her words,
clear my doubts with her advice, and lift my sadness by her
humor. How priceless is a friend whose very look brings comfort.

Thank You for my friend. Bless her, God, as she blesses me.
Keep her safe, guide her, give her endurance,
energy, and patience. Let joy bubble up in her soul
so that it spills over onto others. Amen.

A true friend sticks by us in our joys and sorrows. In good times
and bad, we need friends who will pray for us, listen to us, and lend
a comforting hand and an understanding ear when needed.

BEVERLY LaHaye

Two are better than one.... If either of them falls down,
one can help the other up.

ECCLESIASTES 4:9–10 NIV

I thank You, God in heaven, for friends.
When morning wakes, when daytime ends,
I have the consciousness
of loving hands that touch my own,
of tender glance and gentle tone,
of thoughts that cheer and bless! Amen.

MARGARET E. SANGSTER

prayers

promises

praise

A Marriage Blessing

*We thank You that Your blessing will go down
the years with us as a light on our way, as a benediction
to the home we...establish. May that home always be a haven
of strength and love to all who enter it—our neighbors
and our friends. We thank You.*
Amen.

PETER MARSHALL

So this is my prayer: that your love will flourish and that you will
not only love much but well. Learn to love appropriately. You need to
use your head and test your feelings so that your love is sincere and
intelligent, not sentimental gush. Live a lover's life, circumspect and
exemplary, a life Jesus will be proud of: bountiful in fruits from the soul.

PHILIPPIANS 1:9–11 MSG

I wish you the blessing of God for a good beginning
and a steadfast middle time, and may you hold out until a blessed end,
this all in and through Jesus Christ. Amen.

AMISH BLESSING

He who made them at the beginning "made them male and female,"
and said, "For this reason a man shall leave his father and mother
and be joined to his wife, and the two shall become one flesh."
So then, they are no longer two but one flesh.
Therefore what God has joined together, let not man separate."

MATTHEW 19:4–6 NKJV

prayers

promises

praise

The Church

Thank You, Lord, for my church.
It is more than a building, more than a place to go
once a week to hear an uplifting message. It is a lifeline to You.

My church has arms that reach out to show Your comfort,
legs that take Your Word to the world, lips that sing Your praises.

Lord, bless my church. Bless the leaders, the volunteers,
the people who gather there. Bind us together
into one family through Christ. Make the building we meet
in a place that welcomes and comforts. Bless all who come
through the doors and those who go out from it.

And, Lord, bless all the churches in my community,
my state, my country, the world. As they share Your Word,
bless them so they can be a blessing. Amen.

God has put all things under the authority of Christ
and has made him head over all things for the benefit of the church.
And the church is his body; it is made full and complete by Christ,
who fills all things everywhere with himself.

EPHESIANS 1:22–23 NLT

A room of quiet—a temple of peace;
A home of faith—where doubtings cease;
A house of comfort—where hope is given;
A source of strength—to make earth heaven;
A shrine of worship—a place to pray—
I found all this—in my church today.

ANONYMOUS

prayers

promises

praise

Prayer for Authorities

We pray, dear God,
through whom authority is rightly administered,
laws are enacted, and judgments decreed, that You assist
the authorities in charge over us, that their leadership may
be conducted in righteousness and be eminently useful
to the people over whom they preside. Encourage due respect
for virtue and religion by a faithful execution of the laws
in justice and mercy, and by restraining vice and immorality.
Let the light of Your divine wisdom direct the deliberations
of these authorities and shine through all the proceedings,
that they may tend to the preservation of peace, the promotion
of happiness, and the blessing of equality for all.

PARAPHRASE OF BISHOP JOHN CARROLL'S 1789
"PRAYER FOR AUTHORITIES"

The first thing I want you to do is pray. Pray every way you know how,
for everyone you know. Pray especially for rulers and their governments
to rule well so we can be quietly about our business of living simply, in
humble contemplation. This is the way our Savior God wants us to live.

1 TIMOTHY 2:1–3 MSG

We must pray for those who are in authority over us if we wish
to reap the benefits of good government, which is a prized gift from
God for the church's welfare and advancement of the gospel.

JACK HAYFORD

There is no authority except from God,
and the authorities that exist are appointed by God.

ROMANS 13:1 NKJV

prayers

promises

praise

For Those Far Away

Every time I think of you,
I give thanks to my God. Whenever I pray,
I make my requests for all of you with joy,
for you have been my partners in spreading the Good News
about Christ from the time you first heard it until now.
And I am certain that God, who began the good work within you,
will continue his work until it is finally finished
on the day when Christ Jesus returns.

So it is right that I should feel as I do about all of you,
for you have a special place in my heart. You share with me
the special favor of God.... God knows how much I love you
and long for you with the tender compassion of Christ Jesus.

PHILIPPIANS 1:3-8 NLT

No distance of place or lapse of time
can lessen the friendship
of those who are thoroughly persuaded
of each other's worth.

ROBERT SOUTHEY

Friendship is not diminished by distance
or time...by suffering or silence.
It is in these things that it roots most deeply.
It is from these things that it flowers.

PAM BROWN

prayers

promises

praise

Mentoring Relationships

Lord,
I want my life so consumed by Your love that others see
and feel the difference. When people get close to me and know
my heart, I pray they will see the real deal. Help me to be
authentic about my faith—to live in such a way that my everyday
actions and lifestyle attract others to You. May my walk be worthy
of the gospel. In the name of Jesus Christ I pray. Amen.

DAN BRITTON AND JIMMY PAGE

Whatever you have learned or received or heard from me, or seen in
me—put it into practice. And the God of peace will be with you.

PHILIPPIANS 4:9 NIV

When others don't know how to pray for themselves,
God answers our prayers on their behalf.

JANETTE OKE

Example is not the main thing in influencing others. It is the only thing.

ALBERT SCHWEITZER

Better than a thousand days of diligent study
is one day with a great teacher.

JAPANESE PROVERB

We always thank God for all of you and pray for you constantly.
As we pray to our God and Father about you, we think
of your faithful work, your loving deeds, and the enduring
hope you have because of our Lord Jesus Christ.

1 THESSALONIANS 1:2-3 NLT

prayers

promises

praise

SECTION FOUR
Well-Being & Healing

In the big moments of life, most of us turn to Him. When we are hurting, we are ready and willing to fall on our knees and ask for God's help. He is the great Healer. He wants us to come to Him for comfort, for healing, for strength.

But He also wants us to come to Him with our daily anxieties, our little worries, our irritable attitudes. God wants us to trust Him with the foundation of our well-being—the healthy handling of our daily living. If we can't give Him the little decisions, the frustrations, the finger-chewing anxiety, we won't be able to accept His promises or sing His praises. Daily prayers for help with these issues will bring health to our minds, bodies, and spirits.

Relief from Stress

Dear Lord and Father...
Drop Your still dews of quietness,
Till all our strivings cease;
Take from our souls the strain and stress,
And let our ordered lives confess
The beauty of Your peace.
Breathe through the heats of our desire
Your coolness and Your balm;
Let sense be dumb, let flesh retire;
Speak through the earthquake, wind, and fire,
O still, small voice of calm.

JOHN GREENLEAF WHITTIER

As we practice the presence of God, more and more we find ourselves
going through the stresses and strains of daily activity with an ease
and serenity that amazes even us...especially us.

RICHARD J. FOSTER

Prayer is an essential therapy during stressful times.

CHARLES R. SWINDOLL

When I said, "My foot is slipping,"
your unfailing love, LORD, supported me.
When anxiety was great within me,
your consolation brought me joy.

PSALM 94:18-19 NIV

prayers

promises

praise

A Healthy Attitude

Lord, thank You for Your concern
for my mental well-being. You give hope when
I'm overwhelmed and humility when I'm overly proud.
Lord, I want a good, positive attitude in all areas of my life.

Create in me Jesus' attitude. Help me to think of others' needs,
to not let the daily grind get me down, and to react with patience,
remembering that my hope is eternal. Guard my thoughts and
attitudes. Let thanksgiving and praise come easily to my lips.

My help is in You. All that I have comes from You.
You are with me through any situation. Help me to cling
to that when I'm tempted to let gloominess, grouchiness,
or self-centeredness affect my psychological wellness.
I can conquer my attitude through You. Amen.

Have the same mindset as Christ Jesus:
Who, being in very nature God,
did not consider equality with God something
to be used to his own advantage;
rather, he made himself nothing
by taking the very nature of a servant,
being made in human likeness.
And being found in appearance as a man,
he humbled himself
by becoming obedient to death—
even death on a cross!

PHILIPPIANS 2:5–8 NIV

prayers

promises

praise

Overcoming

God, enable us by Your wisdom
to keep things in perspective.
For, God, You are bigger than the problems we face each day.
We remember Your mercy and faithfulness.
Through Your counsel and encouragement,
You have enabled us to overcome the many setbacks
and adversities of life.

We continue now, to trust in Your goodness and provision.
For You are a God who hears, answers, and acts on our behalf,
Out of the abundance of Your eternal love.
We trust You in Your grace and mercy to sustain us. Amen.

M. Y. Lee

He said not: "You shall not be tempted,
you shall not be fatigued, you shall not be afflicted":
but He said: "You shall not be overcome."

Julian of Norwich

I pray that you may enjoy good health
and that all may go well with you,
even as your soul is getting along well.

3 John 1:2 niv

I have told you these things, so that in me you may have peace.
In this world you will have trouble.
But take heart! I have overcome the world.

John 16:33 niv

prayers

promises

praise

Heal Me

Lord of Mercy and Comfort,
You are the One I turn to for help.
You are always watching out for me.
Please send Your mercy and healing today.
Drive all sickness and weakness
from my body and keep it away.

Lord, please remove my fear and doubt.
Turn my suffering into compassion,
my weakness into strength, my sorrow into joy,
and my pain into comfort. Help me to trust
in Your goodness and hope in Your faithfulness.
Fill me with patience so that even in the middle of my suffering,
Your joy will shine through me.

Renew me and heal me in the name of Jesus Christ. Amen.

Trust in your Redeemer's strength...exercise what faith you have,
and by and by He shall rise upon you with healing beneath His wings.
Go from faith to faith and you shall receive blessing upon blessing.

CHARLES H. SPURGEON

Let all that I am praise the LORD;
may I never forget the good things he does for me.
He forgives all my sins
and heals all my diseases.

PSALM 103:2-3 NLT

prayers

promises

praise

Soothe the Suffering

Tend Your sick ones, O Lord Christ.
Rest Your weary ones.
Bless Your dying ones.
Soothe Your suffering ones.
Pity Your afflicted ones.
Shield Your joyous ones.
And for all Your love's sake.
Amen.

AUGUSTINE

The LORD sustains them on their sickbed
and restores them from their bed of illness.

PSALM 41:3 NIV

God comforts. He doesn't pity. He picks us up,
dries our tears, soothes our fears,
and lifts our thoughts beyond the hurt.

ROBERT SCHULLER

The prayer offered in faith will make the sick person well;
the Lord will raise them up. If they have sinned,
they will be forgiven. Therefore confess your sins to each other
and pray for each other so that you may be healed.
The prayer of a righteous person is powerful and effective.

JAMES 5:15-16 NIV

prayers

promises

praise

Bless the Caregivers

Lord,
You are the Great Physician.
I kneel before You. Since every good and perfect
gift must come from You, I pray:
Give skill to the surgeons' hands and clarity to the nurses
and doctors. Bring sympathy and kindness to the hearts
of all the medical personnel. Give them singleness of purpose,
strength to help lift the burden of suffering, and a true
realization of the rare privilege they have as healers.

Remove from their hearts any guile or worldliness,
so that with the simple faith of a child they may rely
on You for their talent, skill, and decisions. Bless them
with Your peace and guide them to Your will. Amen.

PARAPHRASE OF "A PHYSICIAN'S PRAYER"

I was hungry and you gave me something to eat,
I was thirsty and you gave me something to drink,
I was a stranger and you invited me in,
I needed clothes and you clothed me,
I was sick and you looked after me,
I was in prison and you came to visit me.

MATTHEW 25:35-36 NIV

Blessed are they who tenderly seek to comfort
another and never run out of compassion and grace.

JANET L. SMITH

prayers

promises

praise

Compassion & Comfort

Heavenly Father,
Speak to me today concerning how to reach out to the world.
From the youngest to the oldest, there is something
we all can do. Allow me to set an example of compassion
and concern for others to my children. Amen.

KIM BOYCE

A part of our petition must always be for an increasing
discernment so that we can see things as God sees them.
We may ask for greater faith so that we can heal others,
but God, who understands human need far better than we do,
gives us greater compassion so that we can weep with others.

RICHARD J. FOSTER

I would rather make mistakes in kindness and compassion
than work miracles in unkindness and hardness.

MOTHER TERESA

All praise to the God and Father of our Master,
Jesus the Messiah! Father of all mercy!
God of all healing counsel! He comes alongside
us when we go through hard times,
and before you know it, he brings us
alongside someone else who is going through
hard times so that we can be there for
that person just as God was there for us.

2 CORINTHIANS 1:3-4 MSG

prayers

promises

praise

SECTION FIVE
Protection & Safety

"Keep them safe." That is a universal prayer. We all want our families and friends to be safe. We want to make sure they are protected from whatever evil is out in the world. We form police forces, military outposts, and cutting-edge monitoring systems all for the purpose of keeping those we love safe.

Our first and most important round of defense, however, is always communication with our Father. When we are afraid for ourselves or others, there is nothing more effective than talking with God. A simple prayer for safety, a verbal claim of protection from His Word, praise for watching over us—in these we find security.

God Is for Us

Dear God,
You are the One True God,
all powerful and mighty. There is no one like you.

No one can stand against You. And if You are for me,
no one can successfully come against me.
Some days I am tempted or frightened. But You, God,
are there for me always. You give me a way out
or the strength to get through. Life gives me burdens,
but You replace them with peace. There is no one greater
than You, God. I thank You and praise You
for watching over me. Amen.

Grasp the fact that God is for you—let this certainty make
its impact on you in relation to what you are up against at this very
moment; and you will find in thus knowing God as your sovereign
protector, irrevocably committed to you in the covenant of grace,
both freedom from fear and new strength for the fight.

J. I. PACKER

What, then, shall we say in response to these things?
If God is for us, who can be against us? He who did not spare
his own Son, but gave him up for us all—how will he not also,
along with him, graciously give us all things?

ROMANS 8:31-32 NIV

And if our God is for us, then who could ever stop us
And if our God is with us, then what can stand against?

CHRIS TOMLIN

prayers

promises

praise

God, Our Protector

O God, our help in ages past,
Our hope for years to come,
Our shelter from the stormy blast,
And our eternal home!
Beneath the shadow of Your throne
Still may we dwell secure;
Sufficient is Your arm alone,
And our defense is sure....
A thousand ages in Your sight
Are like an evening gone;
Short as the watch that ends the night
Before the rising sun....
O God our help in ages past,
Our hope for years to come,
God, be our guard while life shall last,
And our eternal home.

ISAAC WATTS

Whoever fears the LORD has a secure fortress,
and for their children it will be a refuge.

PROVERBS 14:26 NIV

When we are told that God, who is our dwelling place, is also our
fortress, it can only mean one thing, and that is, that if we will but live
in our dwelling place, we shall be perfectly safe and secure from every
assault of every possible enemy that can attack us.

HANNAH WHITALL SMITH

prayers

promises

praise

Protect My Family

Father,
I love my family. Thank You for letting me share
life with each one of them. I know that we
are protected by Your impenetrable shield
of care and love. We belong to You. And You always
watch over those who belong to You. Always.

Thank You for faith, Father, that overcomes fear.
You shelter and protect my family no matter what storm
comes our way. Help us to trust the safety of Your arms.
Give us the eternal hope of a life secure in You. Amen.

For whatever life holds for you and your family in the coming days,
weave the unfailing fabric of God's Word through your heart and mind.
It will hold strong, even if the rest of life unravels.

GIGI GRAHAM TCHIVIDJIAN

There is none like the God...
Who rides the heavens to your help,
And through the skies in His majesty.
The eternal God is a dwelling place,
And underneath are the everlasting arms.

DEUTERONOMY 33:26–27 NASB

Prayer is a long-term investment, one that will increase
your sense of security because God is your protector.
Keep at it every day, for prayer is the key of the day
and the bolt of the evening. God is waiting to hear from you.

BARBARA JOHNSON

prayers

promises

praise

Guard My Children

Father God,
thank You for the gift of my children.
They have blessed my life in ways I can't describe or count.
Please watch over them. Place a barrier of protection
around each one right now wherever they may be.
Keep Your angels on guard around them.

Father, protect them from evil. Protect them from natural dangers,
from their own foolishness, and from those who want to harm
them. Keep them from temptation. Shield and watch over them
every moment of every day.

I praise You for the net of safety You provide my children.
Thank You for being awake, watching even when we are asleep.
Your constant protection is a balm to my soul. Amen.

I never cease to pray that God will guard
and keep you safe within His love each day.

JANIE HARPER FORD

Those who respect the Lord will have security,
and their children will be protected.

PROVERBS 14:26 NCV

Thank You, Lord, for loving us unconditionally and for helping us to do
the same for our children. We speak blessings upon all our children,
and we thank You for sending them as blessings to us. Amen.

QUIN SHERRER

prayers

promises

praise

A Secure Home

Peace, unto this house, I pray,
Keep terror and despair away;
Shield it from evil and let sin
Never find lodging room within.
May never in these walls be heard
The hateful or accusing word.
Grant that its warm and mellow light
May be to all a beacon bright,
A flaming symbol that shall stir
The beating pulse of him or her
Who finds this door and seems to say,
"Here end the trials of the day."...
Let Your love and let Your grace
Shine upon our dwelling place.

EDGAR GUEST

The Bible does not say very much about homes;
it says a great deal about the things that make them.
It speaks about life and love and joy and peace and rest.
If we get a house and put these into it, we shall have secured a home.

JOHN HENRY JOWETT

My people will live in safety, quietly at home.
They will be at rest.
Even if the forest should be destroyed
and the city torn down,
the LORD will greatly bless his people.

ISAIAH 32:18–20 NLT

prayers

promises

praise

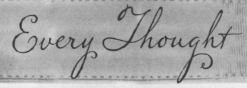

Every Thought

Dear Lord,
We rejoice in You always. Our joy rings from
the rooftops. You are always beside us. We give You our anxiety
about every little thing. For every situation, we come to You
through prayer and petition. With a grateful heart,
we present our requests. We ask that Your peace,
which is beyond our understanding, will protect our hearts
and thoughts through Jesus Christ.

Help us take control of our thoughts. Help us to think about
only what is true, noble, right, pure, lovely, admirable,
excellent, or praiseworthy. We want to think about the things
we have learned from You. Teach us to put a new thought life
into practice. And give us peace. Amen.

PARAPHRASE OF PHILIPPIANS 4:2-9

God's Word acts as a light for our paths. It can help scare off unwanted
thoughts in our minds and protect us from the enemy.

GARY SMALLEY AND JOHN TRENT

We demolish arguments and every pretension
that sets itself up against the knowledge of God,
and we take captive every thought to make it obedient to Christ.

2 CORINTHIANS 10:5 NIV

Begin the day with friendliness
And only friends you'll find.
Yes, greet the dawn with happiness;
Keep happy thoughts in mind.

FRANK B. WHITNEY

prayers

promises

praise

Safe Travels

May it be Your will, Lord my God,
to lead me on the way of peace and guide
and direct my steps in peace, so that You will bring me
happily to my destination, safe and sound. Save me from
danger on the way. Give me good grace, kindness, and favor
in both Your eyes and in the eyes of all whom I may meet.
Hear this my prayer, for You are a God who hears
to the heart's supplication and communion.
Blessed are You, Lord our God, who hears prayer.

PRAYER FOR TRAVELERS

It is God to whom and with whom we travel,
and while He is the End of our journey,
He is also at every stopping place.

ELISABETH ELLIOT

May the road rise to meet you,
May the wind be always at your back,
May the sun shine warm upon your face,
May the rain fall soft upon your fields,
And, until we meet again,
May God hold you in the palm of His hand.

IRISH BLESSING

Wherever you go and whatever you do,
you will be blessed.

DEUTERONOMY 28:6 NLT

prayers

promises

praise

Facing Fears

Father,
I'm up against more than I can handle on my own.
Help me. Show me how to use every weapon You have given me,
so that when it's all said and done I will be standing firm.
Truth, righteousness, and peace are more than words.
They are armor. Your Word is my best weapon. But faith is also
essential in battle. Teach me how to use them effectively.

I will pray hard and long before the battle begins.
I will pray for the safety of my family. I will pray for all Your
people. Help us all to be prepared and alert. Amen.

PARAPHRASE OF EPHESIANS 6:13–18

Come, Thou long-expected Jesus,
Born to set Thy people free;
From our fears and sins release us;
Let us find our rest in Thee.

CHARLES WESLEY

Hope is some extraordinary spiritual grace that
God gives us to control our fears, not to oust them.

VINCENT MCNABB

I sought the LORD, and He heard me,
And delivered me from all my fears.

PSALM 34:4 NKJV

prayers

promises

praise

SECTION SIX
Our Walk with God

In a world that offers distractions of every conceivable type, we often forget how fragile our souls are. They need daily attention, daily filling, a daily infusion of peace. We can get caught between running ourselves ragged and giving up on everything because we are afraid of doing things poorly. Too often our spiritual well-being gets lost in the middle.

Our spirits crave refreshment. Daily nourishment rejuvenates them. Our faith grows and matures when we offer prayers of gratitude, seek God's wisdom, and to invite His presence. Knowing that God cares about everything that concerns us, we can claim His promises and revitalize our souls. As we take the time to seek Him, He will give us the daily guidance, strength, and perseverance we need to refresh our souls.

The Source of All

*Mighty God, Source of strength,
I thank You for Your blessings. Only when walking with You
do I find the courage and wisdom to go through each day.
You fill my life with joy, providing everything I need.*

*God, You are the Source from which radiates joy, comfort,
and grace. When I am tempted to look to others or to my own
efforts for answers, for guidance, for spiritual nourishment,
remind me again that You are all I need. As the Creator
of the universe, You are more than enough. May my contentment
in Your provision bloom and grow into a beautiful,
all-encompassing faith as I walk each day with You. Amen.*

He is the Source of everything. Strength for your day.
Wisdom for your task. Comfort for your soul.
Grace for your battle. Provision for each need.
Understanding for each failure. Assistance for every encounter.

ANONYMOUS

We take our lead from Christ,
who is the source of everything we do.
He keeps us in step with each other.
His very breath and blood flow through us,
nourishing us so that we will grow up
healthy in God, robust in love.

EPHESIANS 4:14 MSG

prayers

promises

praise

Salvation

Jesus,
I come to You asking for the forgiveness of my sins.
I believe with my heart that Jesus is Your Son,
and that He died on the cross at Calvary
that I might be forgiven and have eternal life.
I truly believe that Jesus rose from the dead.

Jesus, I ask You to come into my life
and be my Lord and Savior. I repent of my sins
and will worship You all the days of my life!
Thank You for Your unlimited grace, which saves me
from my sins. I receive Your gift of grace.
Transform my life so that I may bring
glory and honor to You alone.
In Your name, amen.

It is the way of grace. People do not merit salvation
but receive it as a free gift from God on the basis
of what Christ's death accomplished.

LEON MORRIS

If you confess with your mouth that Jesus is Lord
and believe in your heart that God raised him from the dead,
you will be saved. For it is by believing in your heart
that you are made right with God, and it is by confessing
with your mouth that you are saved.

ROMANS 10:9–10 NLT

prayers

promises

praise

A Steadfast Heart

Give us, O Lord,
a steadfast heart,
Which no unworthy affection may drag downwards;
Give us an unconquered heart,
Which no tribulation can wear out;
Give us an upright heart,
Which no unworthy purpose may tempt aside.
Bestow upon us also, O Lord our God,
Understanding to know You,
Diligence to seek You, wisdom to find You,
And a faithfulness that may finally embrace You;
Through Jesus Christ our Lord.

THOMAS AQUINAS

We shall steer safely through every storm,
so long as our heart is right, our intention fervent,
our courage steadfast, and our trust fixed on God.

FRANCIS DE SALES

Create in me a pure heart, O God,
and renew a steadfast spirit within me.
Do not cast me from your presence
or take your Holy Spirit from me.
Restore to me the joy of your salvation
and grant me a willing spirit, to sustain me.

PSALM 51:10-12 NIV

prayers

promises

praise

With Thanksgiving

Accept, O Lord, our thanks and praise
for all that You have done for us. We thank You for
the splendor of the whole creation, for the beauty
of this world, for the wonder of life, and for the mystery of love.
We thank You for the blessing of family and friends,
and for the loving care which surrounds us on every side....

Above all, we thank You for Your Son Jesus Christ;
for the truth of His Word and the example of His life;
for His steadfast obedience, by which He overcame
temptation; for His dying, through which
He overcame death; and for His rising to life again,
in which we are raised to the life of Your kingdom.

Grant us the gift of Your Spirit, that we may know Him
and make Him known; and through Him, at all times
and in all places, may give thanks to You in all things. Amen.

THE BOOK OF COMMON PRAYER

I was lost but now I am found again, Jesus,
and I know what I want: to see deeply, to thank deeply,
to feel joy deeply. How my eyes see, perspective,
is my key to enter into His gates. I only can with thanksgiving.

ANN VOSKAMP

I will praise the name of God with song
And magnify Him with thanksgiving.

PSALM 69:30 NASB

prayers

promises

praise

Let's Pray

O the pure delight of a single hour
that before Your throne I spend,
When I kneel in prayer, and with You, my God,
I commune as friend with friend!

FANNY CROSBY

God is as near as a whispered prayer
No matter the time or place,
Whether skies are blue
And all's right with you,
Or clouds dim the road you face.
In His mercy and great compassion
He will ease, He will help, He will share!
Whatever your lot,
Take heart in the thought:
God's as near as a whispered prayer!

JON GILBERT

I love the LORD because he hears my voice
and my prayer for mercy.
Because he bends down to listen,
I will pray as long as I have breath!

PSALM 116:1-2 NLT

Praise be to God, who has not rejected
my prayer or withheld his love from me!

PSALM 66:20 NIV

prayers

promises

praise

Staying Faithful

Dear Jesus,
At times it has been difficult, but I have fought
the good fight and finished the race. Through it all,
I have kept the faith. I may have wavered, but I did not quit.
Strengthen my faith so it wavers less and less.

To those who stay faithful, You have promised
an eternal reward. I can't wait to see it.
Experiencing Your promises and blessings
increase my faith—and not only mine, but all the others
who have been faithful. You give us eternal hope. Amen.

PARAPHRASE OF 2 TIMOTHY 4:7-8

It is on the unshakable fact of the resurrection of Christ
from the dead that I base my faith in God's utter integrity
and faithfulness. He let Jesus die—but only because
He would raise Him again. You can count on Him! You can stake your
faith on God—the God of Jesus Christ. He will keep His word.

LEIGHTON FORD

We fix our eyes not on what is seen, but on what is unseen,
since what is seen is temporary, but what is unseen is eternal.

2 CORINTHIANS 4:18 NIV

Faith is to believe what we do not see;
and the reward of this faith is to see what we believe.

AUGUSTINE

prayers

promises

praise

God-Given Joy

God give me joy in the common things:
In the dawn that lures, the eve that sings.
In the new grass sparkling after rain,
In the late wind's wild and weird refrain;
In the springtime's spacious field of gold,
In the precious light by winter doled.
God give me joy in the love of friends,
In the dear home talk as summer ends;
In the songs of children, unrestrained;
In the sober wisdom age has gained.
God give me joy in the tasks that press,
In the memories that burn and bless;
In the thought that life has love to spend,
In the faith that God's at journey's end.
God give me hope for each day that springs,
God give me joy in the common things!

THOMAS CURTIS CLARK

As we grow in our capacities to see and enjoy the joys
that God has placed in our lives, life becomes a glorious
experience of discovering His endless wonders.

WENDY MOORE

I pray that God, the source of hope, will fill you completely
with joy and peace because you trust in him. Then you will overflow
with confident hope through the power of the Holy Spirit.

ROMANS 15:13 NLT

prayers

promises

praise

Knowing God

Teach me, O Lord, to do Your will;
teach me to live worthily and humbly in Your sight;
for You are my Wisdom, who know me truly, and who knew me
before the world was made, and before I had my being.

THOMAS À KEMPIS

What matters supremely is not the fact that I know God,
but the larger fact which underlies it—the fact that *He knows me.*
I am graven on the palms of His hands. I am never out of His mind.
All my knowledge of Him depends on His sustained initiative
in knowing me. I know Him because He first knew me,
and continues to know me.

J. I. PACKER

I have not stopped giving thanks for you,
remembering you in my prayers. I keep asking
that the God of our Lord Jesus Christ,
the glorious Father, may give you the Spirit of wisdom
and revelation, so that you may know him better.
I pray that the eyes of your heart may be enlightened
in order that you may know the hope to which he has called you,
the riches of his glorious inheritance in his holy people,
and his incomparably great power for us who believe.

EPHESIANS 1:16-19 NIV

prayers

promises

praise

SECTION SEVEN
Peace & Quiet

Peace. That quiet, calm, opposite-of-anxious feeling that permeates our lives and seeps into our bones. We all want it. We look for peace in many places—in spas, in music, in medicine, in other people.

Fortunately, true peace, satisfying peace, is readily available to all who seek it. It is not found in our earthly pursuits. Genuine peace, that spiritual quietness we crave, exists in just one place—God. To accept this gift, we only need open hands and a trusting heart.

Quieting our spirits and letting God's peace settle over us can be challenging, especially during tough times. That's where prayer comes in. It unlocks the promise of peace.

My Quiet Time

Lord,
I crave my moments of quiet.
I need that time to have a real conversation with You,
to prayerfully consider the responsibilities of the day,
and to recharge my weak batteries. Without that time,
no matter how brief, I have a hard time knowing Your peace.

Lord, remind me to structure my schedule so that I have
time in every day to quiet myself before You. Still my soul.
Please, Lord, give me time to unburden my heart, to share with
You the cries, the praises, the frustrations, and the prayer
for others. I wait in Your presence for direction and wisdom.
Thank You for listening and refreshing my soul. Amen.

So wait before the Lord. Wait in the stillness.
And in that stillness, assurance will come to you.
You will know that you are heard; you will know
that your Lord ponders the voice of your humble desires;
you will hear quiet words spoken to you yourself,
perhaps to your grateful surprise and refreshment.

AMY CARMICHAEL

Quiet down before GOD,
be prayerful before him.

PSALM 37:7 MSG

prayers

promises

praise

Peace Granted

O Lord, my God,
grant us Your peace; already, indeed,
You have made us rich in all things!
Give us that peace of being at rest,
that Sabbath peace,
the peace which knows no end.

AUGUSTINE

Jesus calls to surrender and there's nothing like releasing fears
and falling into peace. It terrifies, true. But it exhilarates.

ANN VOSKAMP

"May peace be within your walls,
And prosperity within your palaces."...
I will now say, "May peace be within you."
For the sake of the house of the LORD our God,
I will seek your good.

PSALM 122:7-9 NASB

The LORD bless you and keep you;
the LORD make his face shine on you
and be gracious to you;
the LORD turn his face toward you
and give you peace.

NUMBERS 6:24-26 NIV

prayers

promises

praise

Anger Stilled

Lord God,
please forgive me for letting my anger
get the best of me. Please bring healing and restoration
to the areas that have been damaged or hurt because of anger.
Search my heart! Guide me! Still my tongue when my anger feels
out of control. Help me to quiet my emotions and lean on You.

Likewise, help those around me lean on You and deal
with their anger in a godly way, in quiet patience. Amen.

Be slow to anger, slow to blame,
And slow to plead your cause.
But swift to speak of any gain
That gives your friend applause.

MARY WHITCHER

When times get hard, remember Jesus. When people don't listen,
remember Jesus. When tears come, remember Jesus.
When disappointment is your bedpartner, remember Jesus.
When fear pitches his tent in your front yard. When death looms,
when anger singes, when shame weighs heavily. Remember Jesus.

MAX LUCADO

"Don't sin by letting anger control you."
Don't let the sun go down while you are still angry.

EPHESIANS 4:26 NLT

Be still, and know that I am God.

PSALM 46:10 NIV

prayers

promises

praise

Calm in the Storm

Calm me, O Lord, as You stilled the storm,
Still me, O Lord, keep me from harm.
Let all the tumult within me cease,
Enfold me, Lord, in Your peace.

CELTIC TRADITIONAL

The lightning and thunder,
They go and they come,
But the stars and the stillness
Are always at home.

GEORGE MACDONALD

Then they cried out to the LORD in their trouble,
and he brought them out of their distress.
He stilled the storm to a whisper;
the waves of the sea were hushed.
They were glad when it grew calm.

PSALM 107:28–30 NIV

Only Christ Himself, who slept in the boat in the storm
and then spoke calm to the wind and waves,
can stand beside us when we are in a panic
and say to us Peace. It will not be explainable.
It transcends human understanding.
And there is nothing else like it in the whole wide world.

ELISABETH ELLIOT

prayers

promises

praise

Source of Peace

Lord,
make me an instrument of Your peace;
where there is hatred, let me sow love;
where there is injury, pardon;
where there is doubt, faith;
where there is despair, hope;
where there is darkness, light;
and where there is sadness, joy.
Amen.

FRANCIS OF ASSISI

Therefore, having been justified by faith,
we have peace with God through our Lord Jesus Christ,
through whom also we have obtained our introduction
by faith into this grace in which we stand;
and we exult in hope of the glory of God.

ROMANS 5:1-2 NASB

Peace I leave with you; my peace I give you.
I do not give to you as the world gives. Do not let your hearts
be troubled and do not be afraid.

JOHN 14:27 NIV

Let's praise His name! He is holy, He is almighty.
He is love. He brings hope, forgiveness, heart cleansing,
peace and power. He is our deliverer and coming King.
Praise His wonderful name!

LUCILLE M. LAW

prayers

promises

praise

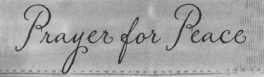

Prayer for Peace

Dear Jesus,
hear my prayers. Bring peace to my family,
my friends, and those who are dearest to me.
In the chaos that sometimes rules our lives,
we need the soothing stillness of Your voice.
Help every breath be a prayer of peace,
every action be reflection of Your serenity.
Bring us fully into Your presence
as we intercede daily for peace. Amen.

Unceasing prayer has a way of speaking peace to the chaos.
Our fractured and fragmented activities begin focusing
around a new Center of Reference. We experience peace,
stillness, serenity, firmness of life orientation.

RICHARD J. FOSTER

I urge you, first of all, to pray for all people.
Ask God to help them; intercede on their behalf, and give thanks
for them...so that we can live peaceful and quiet lives marked
by godliness and dignity. This is good and pleases God our Savior,
who wants everyone to be saved and to understand the truth.

I TIMOTHY 2:1-4 NLT

Speak, move, act in peace, as if you were in prayer.
In truth, this is prayer.

FRANÇOIS FÉNELON

prayers

promises

praise

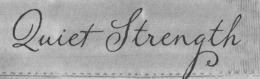

Quiet Strength

O God of peace,
who has taught us that in returning and rest
we shall be saved, in quietness and confidence
shall be our strength: by the might of Your Spirit
lift us, we pray to You, to Your presence,
where we may be still and know that You are God;
through Jesus Christ our Lord. Amen.

THE BOOK OF COMMON PRAYER

Let your faith in Christ, the omnipresent One,
be in the quiet confidence that He will every day
and every moment keep you as the apple of His eye,
keep you in perfect peace and in the sure experience
of all the light and the strength you need in His service.

ANDREW MURRAY

In repentance and rest is your salvation,
in quietness and trust is your strength....
Yet the LORD longs to be gracious to you;
therefore he will rise up to show you compassion.
For the LORD is a God of justice.
Blessed are all who wait for him!

ISAIAH 30:15, 18 NIV

prayers

promises

praise

SECTION EIGHT

Strength & Perseverance

Some days we feel too weak to microwave popcorn, much less do our jobs, raise our children, or mentor someone through a difficult time. We need an infusion of strength. We need stability and confidence and grit. That kind of strength and perseverance doesn't come from within us, it comes from Jesus.

We can tap into His strength every day, every minute. When we have nothing left, His promises hold us securely. He is big enough for our problems, our worries, and our doubts. He takes weakness and transforms it into something beautifully strong. He carries us so we can carry others.

God's Strength

Father,
Everyone thinks that I am so strong,
but I'm not as strong as they think. In fact,
I am alarmingly close to completely falling apart.
Without You I have no strength at all! Hold me together.
Renew my resolve. I seek refuge in You.

You have the power to overcome all. You conquer
every trouble. Your strength always prevails.
I praise You, Father, that through You,
I also will prevail. Your strength is my strength
and for that I am eternally grateful. Amen.

I don't think there is anyone who needs God's help
and grace as much as I do. Sometimes I feel so helpless and weak.
I think that is why God uses me. Because I cannot depend
on my own strength, I rely on Him twenty-four hours a day.

MOTHER TERESA

God is our refuge and strength,
A very present help in trouble.
Therefore we will not fear,
though the earth should change
And though the mountains slip
into the heart of the sea.

PSALM 46:1–3 NASB

prayers

promises

praise

Overcomers

Remember, Lord, my faithful
and wholehearted devotion to You?
Remember how I have done good in your eyes?
Hear my prayer. Witness my tears. I need Your help.

You are the great Overcomer. You have promised
that with Your help I can also be an overcomer.
You have promised a way through my troubles.
I cling to that promise right now. I believe in You.
I am not asking for my problems to disappear.
I am simply claiming Your promise that if I have faith,
You will overcome any problem. Lord, I have faith.
Make me an overcomer. Amen.

Christ desires to be with you in whatever crisis you
may find yourself. Call upon His name.
See if He will not do as He promised He would.
He will not make your problems go away, but He will give
you the power to deal with and overcome them.

BILLY GRAHAM

You...are from God and have overcome them,
because the one who is in you is greater
than the one who is in the world.

1 JOHN 4:4 NIV

prayers

promises

praise

Perseverance

Father in heaven,
Thank You for not giving up on me.
All along You've kept patiently bringing me back
to Your presence. Now I realize that next to You
is where I want to be.

Father, give me perseverance
in what I am dealing with today. Help me to ask
and keep asking, to knock and keep knocking—even when it
seems no one will answer. I have faith that the door
will open in Your time and that until then,
You will give me the strength to keep going.
With You by my side, I will persevere. Amen.

'Tis a lesson you should heed,
Try, try again;
If at first you don't succeed,
Try, try again;
Then your courage should appear,
For, if you will persevere,
You will conquer, never fear;
Try, try again.

W. E. HICKSON

Keep on asking, and you will receive what you ask for. Keep on seeking,
and you will find. Keep on knocking, and the door will be opened to you.
For everyone who asks, receives. Everyone who seeks, finds.
And to everyone who knocks, the door will be opened.

MATTHEW 7:7-8 NLT

prayers

promises

praise

Courage

Jesus,
I do not pray to be sheltered from all dangers,
but instead to have courage to face them.
I do not ask for the absence of pain,
but for the strength to endure it.
Let me not solicit friends to fight my battles,
but depend on You to provide the weapons for success.

Jesus, steer me safely through the storms.
Give me the courage to face my fears
and make godly choices, to stand firm,
knowing that You are on my side.
Thank You for holding me steady when
I would rather run away. Give me not the easy path,
but the endurance to travel the difficult one. Amen.

We walk without fear, full of hope and courage and strength
to do His will, waiting for the endless good which He is always
giving as fast as He can get us able to take it in.

GEORGE MACDONALD

Be strong and courageous. Do not be afraid or terrified
because of them, for the LORD your God goes with you;
he will never leave you nor forsake you.

DEUTERONOMY 31:6 NIV

prayers

promises

praise

Victory

Lord,
remind me that You are the victor.
Sometimes I forget that You are superior to the problems
of my day, that You can turn my weakness into triumph.

Build my strength by showing me how far I've come.
When I am disappointed, angry, or feeling like a failure,
use my past to encourage my future. Through Your help,
I have persevered. I have clothed myself with courage
and I have found victory. Thank You. Amen.

They have had their victories; and when the stress is hardest,
it is wise to look back on these for encouragement. Songs of joy a
nd triumph bring strength and support along a path beset with pain
and sorrow and disappointments. When seen in their true proportions,
these are only faint specks showing in a universe of infinite light.

LAURENCE OLIPHANT

From now on my soul should fight with the prestige of victory,
with the courage that comes of having tried and won,
trusted and not been confounded.

JULIANA H. EWING

Despite all these things, overwhelming victory is ours
through Christ, who loved us. And I am convinced
that nothing can ever separate us from God's love.

ROMANS 8:37-38 NLT

prayers

promises

praise

Temptation

Lord,
as I face everyday temptations,
strengthen me so I am able to say no!
Teach me to be persistent and to turn away
from temptation as it plagues me again and again.
Lord, help me not to be blinded by my wants
and desires or by my need to be like everybody else.
Help me to be different. Help me to stand firm,
even if I stand by myself. For in truth I am never alone—
You are always with me. Amen.

God is faithful; he will not let you be tempted beyond
what you can bear. But when you are tempted,
he will also provide a way out so that you can endure it.

1 CORINTHIANS 10:13 NIV

Swim through your temptations and troubles.
Run to the promises, they [are] our Lord's branches hanging
over the water so that His...children may take a grip of them.

SAMUEL RUTHERFORD

Thanks be to God! He gives us the victory
through our Lord Jesus Christ. Therefore,
my dear brothers and sisters, stand firm.
Let nothing move you. Always give yourselves fully
to the work of the Lord, because you know that
your labor in the Lord is not in vain.

1 CORINTHIANS 15:57–58 NIV

prayers

promises

praise

Endurance

We have not stopped praying for you
since we first heard about you. We ask God
to give you complete knowledge of his will
and to give you spiritual wisdom and understanding.
Then the way you live will always honor
and please the Lord, and your lives will produce
every kind of good fruit. All the while,
you will grow as you learn to know God better and better.

We also pray that you will be strengthened
with all his glorious power so you will have
all the endurance and patience you need.
May you be filled with joy, always thanking the Father.
He has enabled you to share in the inheritance
that belongs to his people, who live in the light.

COLOSSIANS 1:9–12 NLT

Jesus doesn't say, "If you succeed you will be saved."
Or, "If you come out on top you will be saved."
He says, "If you endure." An accurate rendering would be,
"If you hang in there until the end...if you go the distance."

MAX LUCADO

But he who endures to the end shall be saved.

MATTHEW 24:13 NKJV

prayers

promises

praise

Encouragement

Dear Lord,
Strengthen me. Refresh me with Your Spirit.
Fill my heart with so much encouragement
that it spills over, splashing onto all those around me.
Use me to build them up, inspiring them to be all You made
them to be, helping them gather strength from trusting You.

Lord, You are awesome. Your Word, Your creation, the
relationships You bring into my life encourage my soul daily.
You are my guiding light. Thank You. Amen.

The God who created the vast resources of the universe is also the
inventor of the human mind. His inspired words of encouragement
guarantee us that we can live above our circumstances.

DR. JAMES DOBSON

Encouragement is oxygen to the soul.

GEORGE M. ADAMS

Encouragement is awesome. It has the capacity to lift
a man's or woman's shoulders. To spark the flicker of a smile
on the face of a discouraged child. To breathe fresh fire
into the fading embers of a smoldering dream. To actually change
the course of another human being's day, week, or life.

CHARLES R. SWINDOLL

Therefore encourage one another and build
each other up, just as in fact you are doing.

1 THESSALONIANS 5:11 NIV

prayers

promises

praise

SECTION NINE

The Work of My Hands

All the work we do is an offering to God. Our career, housekeeping, childrearing, church work. *All* of it. That means we should work for a difficult boss with the same care and efficiency that we would give to building a business for God. We should volunteer to help our neighbors as if it were God Himself who lived next door.

With prayer and patience, our work can reflect the heart of Jesus—a servant's heart. In our careers, in our church, in our day-to-day lives, in all the work we do, Jesus can use our hands to be His hands. His imprint on our lives can be seen through our actions. When we work with integrity, encourage others, volunteer unselfishly, and lead by example, we reflect God's glory. Through the work of our hands, God fulfills His promises.

Working for the Lord

Jesus,
May the work of my hands—
whatever that work may be—bring glory to Your name.
Lord, help me put my whole heart into it.
Let even the most mundane part of my workday
be done with excellence. I give You praise for the work
that I am privileged to do, remembering that it is part
of the ministry You have given me.

Jesus, I offer all my work to You. Thank You for
the opportunity to do it and the skill to perform it.
Thank You for the chance to serve You in this one thing.
Lord, please bless the work of my hands. Amen.

My vocation is grounded in belonging to Jesus,
and in the firm conviction that nothing will separate me
from the love of Christ. The important thing is not how much
we accomplish, but how much love we put into our deeds every day.
That is the measure of our love for God.

MOTHER TERESA

Whatever you do, work at it with all your heart,
as working for the Lord, not for human masters,
since you know that you will receive an inheritance from
the Lord as a reward. It is the Lord Christ you are serving.

COLOSSIANS 3:23-24 NIV

prayers

promises

praise

Work in Me

Lord,
I freely yield all my freedom to You.
Take my memory, my intellect, and my entire will.
You have given me anything I am or have;
I give it all back to You to stand under Your will alone.
Your love and Your grace are enough for me;
I shall ask for nothing more.

IGNATIUS OF LOYOLA

For this reason I bow my knees to the Father
of our Lord Jesus Christ, from whom the whole family
in heaven and earth is named, that He would grant you,
according to the riches of His glory, to be strengthened
with might through His Spirit in the inner man,
that Christ may dwell in your hearts through faith; that you,
being rooted and grounded in love, may be able to comprehend
with all the saints what is the width and length and depth
and height—to know the love of Christ which passes knowledge;
that you may be filled with all the fullness of God.

Now to Him who is able to do exceedingly abundantly
above all that we ask or think, according to the power
that works in us, to Him be glory in the church by Christ Jesus
to all generations, forever and ever. Amen.

EPHESIANS 3:14–21 NKJV

prayers

promises

praise

God-Given Dreams

Lord,
You have given me a desire
to accomplish great things. You have placed
dreams in my heart. Thank You for trusting me
with these dreams, for growing them, for putting
other people in my life who contribute to them.
The way You see the big picture amazes me.
I'm thinking about today and You are preparing my future.
You are always thinking of me!

Lord, make me worthy of the dreams
You have prepared. I'm willing to work hard
to make them come true. Remind me to unceasingly
consult You on how to move forward. Open my mind
to the possibilities and give me the strength to do
what needs to be done, to accomplish
what You have planned. I love You, Lord. Amen.

Allow your dreams a place in your prayers and plans.
God-given dreams can help you move
into the future He is preparing for you.

BARBARA JOHNSON

No eye has seen, no ear has heard,
and no mind has imagined
what God has prepared
for those who love him.

1 CORINTHIANS 2:9 NLT

prayers

promises

praise

Risk Taking

Disturb us, Lord, when
We are too well pleased with ourselves,
When our dreams have come true
Because we have dreamed too little,
When we arrived safely
Because we sailed too close to the shore....
Disturb us, Lord, to dare more boldly,
To venture on wider seas
Where storms will show Your mastery;
Where losing sight of land,
We shall find the stars.
We ask You to push back
The horizons of our hopes;
And to push into the future
In strength, courage, hope, and love.

Sir Francis Drake

He said, "That's what I mean: Risk your life and get more than
you ever dreamed of. Play it safe and end up holding the bag."

Luke 19:26 MSG

The Promised Land belongs to the person who takes the risks,
whose face is marred by dust and sweat,
who strives valiantly while daring everything.

Tony Campolo

Only those who will risk going too far
can possibly find out how far one can go.

T. S. Eliot

prayers

promises

praise

Learning from Failure

Almighty God,
thank You for the job of this day. May we find gladness
in all its toil and difficulty, its pleasure and success,
and even in its failure and sorrow.

We would look always away from ourselves,
and behold the glory and the need of the world
that we may have the will and the strength to bring
the gift of gladness to others; that with them
we stand to bear the burden and heat of the day
and offer You the praise of work well done. Amen.

CHARLES LEWIS SLATTERY

Don't be discouraged by a failure. It can be a positive experience.
Failure is, in a sense, the highway to success,
inasmuch as every discovery of what is false leads us to seek
earnestly after what is true, and every fresh experience points
out some form of error which we shall afterwards carefully avoid.

JOHN KEATS

We were crushed and overwhelmed beyond our ability to endure,
and we thought we would never live through it. In fact, we expected
to die. But as a result, we stopped relying on ourselves and learned to
rely only on God, who raises the dead. And he did rescue us from
mortal danger, and he will rescue us again. We have placed our
confidence in him, and he will continue to rescue us.

2 CORINTHIANS 1:8–10 NLT

prayers

promises

praise

Good Character

Dear God,
Help me put on the mind of Christ
as I go through my day. Remind me that my actions
are the only example of Christ's love that many people will see.
May they find no malice in me, no puffed up pride.
Build my character so that it adequately reflects You.
Shape my character to reflect spiritual understanding,
discipline, patience, self-control, perseverance, and godliness.
In Jesus' name I pray, amen.

So don't lose a minute in building on what you've been given,
complementing your basic faith with good character,
spiritual understanding, alert discipline, passionate patience,
reverent wonder, warm friendliness, and generous love,
each dimension fitting into and developing the others.

2 PETER 1:5-7 MSG

Do you know the greatest message we can deliver?
It is the message of Christlike character. No message on earth
is more needed or more powerful. You want to impact your family...
your church...your community...your place of employment?
You want to make a difference in the life of your mate,
a family member, a friend (Christian or not), some person
in the workplace? Demonstrate the characteristics of Christ.

CHARLES R. SWINDOLL

prayers

promises

praise

Pushes and Shoves

Dearest God,
Nudge me today toward accomplishing Your work.
Keep my hands busy doing what You would have me to do.
When I get off task or start down a wrong path,
God, I am trusting You to set me straight.

God, don't let me get hung up on doing the big,
important things in life, at the expense of ignoring
the essential, detailed work. If I forget, push me back
to reality. Shove me if You have to. Doing well any job
You give me to do brings healthy pride and satisfaction.
Help me to be content in doing Your work. Amen.

Always give yourselves fully to the work of the Lord,
because you know that your labor in the Lord is not in vain.

1 CORINTHIANS 15:58 NIV

I long to accomplish a great and noble task, but it is my chief duty to
accomplish humble tasks as though they were great and noble.
The world is moved along, not only by the mighty shoves of its heroes,
but also by the aggregate of the tiny pushes of each honest worker.

HELEN KELLER

The dream begins, most of the time, with a teacher who believes in you,
who tugs and pushes and leads you on to the next plateau,
sometimes poking you with a sharp stick called truth.

DAN RATHER

prayers

promises

praise

Ellie Claire™ Gift & Paper Corp.
Minneapolis, MN 55337
www.ellieclaire.com

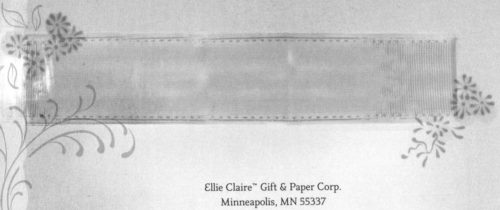

My Quiet Time
Journal
© 2011 by Ellie Claire Gift & Paper Corp.

ISBN 978-1-60936-243-0

Compiled and unattributed prayers written by Marilyn Jansen.
Cover and interior design by Jenny Bethke.

Printed in China.